Fearon Teacher Aids

Adventures with Logic

Mark Schoenfield
and
Jeannette Rosenblatt

Reproducible activities for grades 5-7

For Josh

Cover and interior design: Walt Shelly
Illustrations: Walt Shelly, Bob Morrison

This Fearon Teacher Aids product was formerly manufactured and distributed by American Teaching Aids. Inc., a subsidiary of Silver Burdett Ginn, and is now manufactured and distributed by Frank Schaffer Publications, Inc. FEARON, FEARON TEACHER AIDS, and the FEARON balloon logo are marks used under license from Simon & Schuster, Inc.

© **Fearon Teacher Aids**
A Division of Frank Schaffer Publications, Inc.
23740 Hawthorne Boulevard
Torrance, CA 90505-5927

ISBN-0-8224-0285-8
Printed in the United States of America

CONTENTS

INTRODUCTION

This is not a book in formal logic, but a book that reinforces logical thinking as a practical tool in a student's academic and personal life. Deduction is necessary for scientific experiments, analysis permits the student to intelligently evaluate changing current events, and induction opens the door to a broader understanding of mathematics. And, most important, logic provides the clarity of thought that allows people to communicate effectively, discover new concepts, and test the validity of information that they receive through the media and from people around them.

The activities in this book are divided into five categories: Sequencing, Inference, Deduction, Creative Logic, and Games for Pairs. Each section has an introduction that outlines the activities in the section and offers suggestions for follow-ups and class discussion. An answer key is in the back of the book.

There are several ways that this book can be used in the classroom. Individuals or pairs can work through the activities with minimal supervision, or the entire class may participate. When students work together to solve logical puzzles, they begin to learn alternative strategies from other students. In situations where a student gives up or fails when working alone, the pair or group may succeed. Thus a potential disappointment can be replaced by a confidence building experience.

Each section is arranged in order of difficulty. The activities may be used in sequence, a few per week, or the activities can be given in a more flexible fashion, according to specific needs of the students. Students who finish other work early can be rewarded with an activity page, while the other students continue with their work.

Students have a practical understanding of logic that they have developed in order to function in society and the natural world. This book reinforces rational skills by applying them to fun situations, and helps students become aware of the way they think.

SEQUENCING, SETS, AND ANALOGIES

The classification systems of science, the genres of literature, and the rules of grammar all stem from the recognition of patterns and relationships. The activities in this section present sets and analogies as ways of structuring information.

Moving Day, The Tool Tour, Newspaper Tangle, and Twisted Stories: Students will practice temporal sequencing. A class discussion topic to reinforce this skill could be an exploration of sequencing in the students' personal lives (for example, getting ready for school). Discuss which sequences are crucial and which can be transposed.

Family Set, Animal Set, and Circle Set: Students will practice the rudiments of set theory. This skill is essential in preparation for the mathematics they will encounter in later grades. A class discussion of sets could focus on science (for example, acids/bases, simple machines/complex machines), social studies (explorers/conquerors, mineral-rich countries/agriculturally-rich countries), or any appropriate subject.

Analogies I and II: Students will practice a simple version of SAT-type analogies. In class discussion, students can describe how analogous words are related, and discover the subtle relationships that exist between words.

Moving Day

Two movers, Vicki and Jerry, want to unload their truck efficiently. Some of the furniture is heavy, and they must work together to move it. Read the following rules and the list of items to be moved. Then, write a moving schedule on the bottom of the page.

Rules

1. Vicki and Jerry want to be finished in no more than two hours.

2. They can do different one-person jobs at the same time.

3. The living room paintings must be hung after all of the living room furniture is moved in.

4. Vicki wants to start by carrying in the books, and finish by moving the dining room table.

One-mover Jobs	Time	Two-mover Jobs	Time
Carry in boxes of books	10 min.	Move living room piano	20 min.
Set up living room lamps	20 min.	Move dining room table	20 min.
Set up dining room chairs	20 min.	Move living room sofa	10 min.
Shelve boxes of dishes	20 min.		
Set up bed and headboard	30 min.		
Hang living room paintings	40 min.		

Schedule

Vicki's Jobs	Two-mover Jobs	Jerry's Jobs
_____	_____	_____
_____	_____	_____
_____	_____	_____
_____	_____	_____
_____	_____	_____
_____	_____	_____

Name _____

The Tool Tour

Plan the next tour for the *Tools,* a new rock group. Read the tour requirements below. The mileage map is your guide for distances between cities. On a separate piece of paper, make a calendar and plan the dates for each concert on the tour.

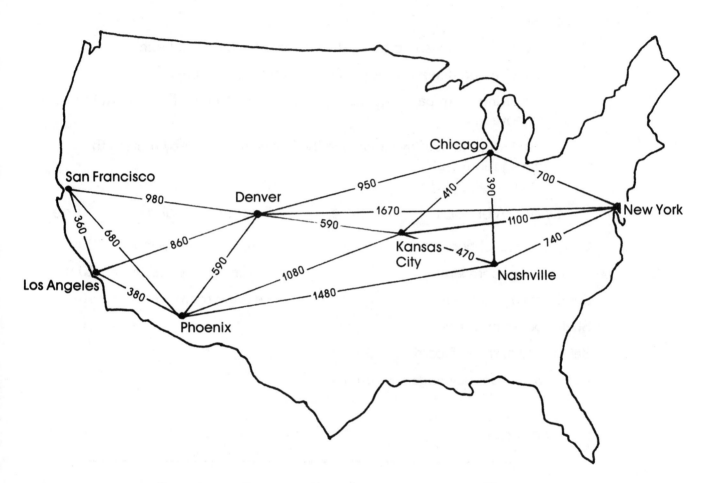

Requirements

1. They want to play in eight cities: Chicago, Denver, Kansas City, Los Angeles, Nashville, New York, Phoenix, and San Francisco.

2. The tour will begin on Monday, July 2, in New York.

3. The tour will end on Sunday, July 29, in Los Angeles.

4. The *Tools* want to travel less than 4,200 miles.

5. In each city, they will perform for two or three days.

6. After each set of concerts in a city, they need at least one day for travel to the next city.

7. They want to have Saturday night concerts in Nashville, San Francisco, and Los Angeles.

Name _____

Newspaper Tangle

Two reporters wired their news stories to the *Science Reporter* at the same time. The two stories were mistakenly mixed together by the computer. The sentences for both stories are in the correct order, but they need to be sorted out. Read the tangled stories below and, on a separate piece of paper, write the two newspaper articles.

The Tangled Stories

NASA expects, once again, to launch the Space Shuttle near dawn this Thursday. A weather satellite is malfunctioning as a result of a computer error, the Weather Service announced today. The satellite provides pictures of the southwestern United States, and is important for predicting changes in air temperature and pressure. The earlier computer problems that threatened to delay the launch have been fixed. The Weather Service believes the malfunction can be fixed in the next few days. "Everything, including the weather, looks good," said launch engineer Marshall Peters. The Space Shuttle will be taking photographs of the sun for scientists to study. Until then, balloons and other older methods will be used. "At least this isn't the rainy season," commented one meteorologist. The photos might help show a relationship between sunspots and weather patterns.

Name _____ 5

Twisted Stories

Two reporters wired their news stories to the *Daily Gazette* at the same time. Unfortunately, the stories were scrambled by the computer. Read the sentences below. On a separate piece of paper, write the two original stories with the sentences in the correct order.

The Twisted Stories

By 10:00 a.m., the flames dwindled, and several volunteers offered temporary shelter for the shop's dogs, cats, snakes, and rabbits. Rescue and observation teams, who had been expecting the eruption for several weeks, moved quickly to evacuate the area. She also reported that many wild deer and squirrels had fled through the nearby town to safety. Early this morning, before the stores opened, a fire broke out in the Center City shopping mall. According to Sue Landoni, the evacuation director, by 3:30 a.m., everyone had been successfully relocated. After the fire was out, Mr. Lansing said, "I think I was more frightened than were the trapped pets." Within minutes, the lava had spread over a 200-acre area, endangering hundreds of families and countless forest animals. Fire trucks rushed to the scene, after the fire was discovered by Larry Lansing, a pastry shop owner. Shortly after 2:00 a.m. this morning, the ancient volcano Quixtola erupted. Although no people were inside, the fire fighters used axes to get to animals trapped in a pet shop.

6   Name _____

Family Set

A *set* is a group of people, things, or words that all have something in common. For example, the *set* "car drivers" is made up of anyone who drives a car.

1. Describe who would be in the *set* "children." _____

   _____

2. Name three animals that would be in the *set* "dogs."

   _____

Each thing in a *set* is called a *member* of that *set*. For example, a hamster is a *member* of the *set* "animals."

3. Name three *members* of the *set* "crawling animals." _____

   _____

4. Monopoly, chess, and rugby are *members* of what *set*? _____

Sometimes a whole *set* will fit inside of another *set*. For example, the *set* "mothers" is included in the *set* "parents," since all mothers are also parents. Because of this, the *set* "mothers" is called a *subset* of the *set* "parents."

5. Name another *subset* of the *set* "parents." _____

6. Why would the *set* "mothers" be a *subset* of the *set*

   "daughters?" _____

7. Would the *set* "daughters" be a *subset* of the *set*

   "mothers?" _____

Sometimes only part of one *set* will be inside another *set*. For example, some *members* of the *set* "daughters" are in the *set* "parents," but some daughters are not parents. When *sets* have only some *members* in common they are called *intersecting sets*.

8. Would the *set* "sons" and the *set* "parents" be *intersecting sets*?

   _____

9. Would the *set* "sons" and the *set* "daughters" be *intersecting sets*?

   _____

Animal Set

Sometimes a circle is used to represent a *set*. A circle inside a larger circle is a *subset* of the larger circle. Two circles which intersect represent *intersecting sets*.

In Diagram 1, the *set* "collies" is shown as a *subset* of "dogs." Label the circles in Diagram 2 to show the relationship between the *set* "whales" and the *set* "swimming animals."

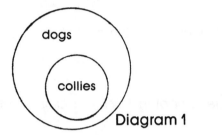

Diagram 1

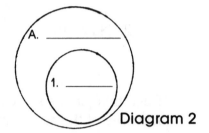

A. _____

1. _____

Diagram 2

In Diagram 3, the *set* "movie actors" intersects with the *set* "millionaires." Some people belong in both *sets* and some belong in one *set* and not the other. Label the circles in Diagram 4 to show the relationship between the *set* "women" and the *set* "basketball players."

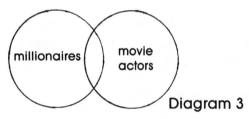

Diagram 3

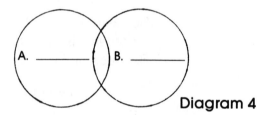

A. _____   B. _____

Diagram 4

In Diagram 5, each circle represents one of these *sets:* "animals," "humans," "males," "females," "men," and "women." The *set* "males" is labeled for you. Label the other five circles.

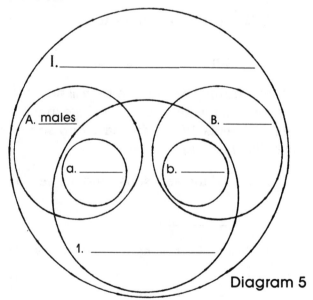

I. _____

A. males   B. _____

a. _____   b. _____

1. _____

Diagram 5

Name _____

Circle Set

Below are two lists of items. For each list, draw circles to represent each item as a *set, subset,* or *intersecting set.* A circle is a *set,* a circle inside another circle is a *subset,* and two intersecting circles are *intersecting sets.* The relationship of all of the items to each other should be shown in one drawing with each circle labeled for the item it represents.

List 1. insects, cats, land creatures, fish, mammals, sharks, water creatures, whales, horses, spiders.

List 2. novels, encyclopedias, non-fiction, paperbacks, fiction, books, dictionaries, science fiction stories.

Name _____

Analogies I

Each sentence below is an analogy with one word missing. Read the sentence and the four words below it. Then, fill in the blank so that the last two underlined words have the same relationship to each other as the first two underlined words.

1. Car is to road as train is to _____.

   a. engine   b. track   c. path   d. passenger

2. President is to nation as _____ is to city.

   a. state   b. mayor   c. governor   d. law

3. _____ is to yard as liter is to quart.

   a. measurement   b. distance   c. meter   d. pound

4. Solar system is to galaxy as city is to _____.

   a. boundaries   b. county   c. courthouse   d. sun

5. Rake is to _____ as mow is to grass.

   a. trees   b. fall   c. leaves   d. pile

6. Joke is to _____ as musical is to finale.

   a. laughter   b. story   c. punchline   d. funny

7. Zoologist is to lion as botanist is to _____.

   a. fern   b. plant   c. roots   d. laboratory

8. Morsel is to food as _____ is to drink.

   a. pour   b. sip   c. thirst   d. milk

9. Blade is to grass as _____ is to corn.

   a. knife   b. stalk   c. kernel   d. field

10. _____ is to snow as rockslide is to rocks.

   a. flake   b. melt   c. winter   d. avalanche

Name _____

Analogies II

For each analogy below, fill in the word that best completes the sentence.

1. Pump is to water as heart is to _____.

2. Knockout is to boxing as checkmate is to _____.

3. Barometer is to air pressure as thermometer is to _____.

4. Stable is to horse as coop is to _____.

5. See is to eye as taste is to _____.

6. Letter is to writing as telephone is to _____.

7. Kennel is to dog as garage is to _____.

8. Winter is to spring as spring is to _____.

For each sentence below, make up two words that have the same relationship to each other as the first two underlined words.

1. Chapter is to book as _____ is to _____.

2. Helmet is to football as _____ is to _____.

3. Evergreen is to tree as _____ is to _____.

4. Paint is to picture as _____ is to _____.

5. Swimming is to pool as _____ is to _____.

6. Mug is to coffee as _____ is to _____.

7. Buy is to store as _____ is to _____.

8. Friend is to like as _____ is to _____.

Name _____

INFERENCE

The use of inference ranges from mathematical problems with only one solution to historical and creative problems with infinite possibilities.

Birthday Surprise, Careful Notes, and Pickle Riddle: Students will infer what the secret code words are, based on the context within each sentence. If these problems are solved as a class activity, have the students explain their guessing process.

A Platter of Plates and Car Appeal: Students will infer the meaning of a code in the form of personalized license plates. There are several possible solutions for some of these activities.

Bottled Code and Post Code: Students will discover the hidden message by manipulating letters according to a set of rules.

Roman Rules, Sporting Chance, Password, and Word Transform: Students will develop strategies to infer the steps necessary to transform words, symbols, and ideas following predetermined rules.

Birthday Surprise

In each set of sentences below, find the secret word that "surprise" replaces. It replaces the same word in all four sentences of a set. However, the secret word is different for each set. After you decode the three secret words, discover the birthday surprise by completing the sentence at the bottom of the page.

Set One

1. We picked up our airplane "surprise" an hour before the flight.
2. I received a parking "surprise" for parking in a no-parking zone.
3. Did you save your "surprise" stub from the movie?
4. I could not get a "surprise" for the play.

surprise = _____

Set Two

1. At the party, everyone had a "surprise."
2. The seal balanced the red "surprise" for almost a minute.
3. The committee organized a charity "surprise" to raise money.
4. I made the snowman's head the size of a bowling "surprise."

surprise = _____

Set Three

1. Ten people were photographing "surprise" on the jungle safari.
2. The "surprise" was called off because of rain.
3. "Crazy eights" is my favorite card "surprise."
4. Chess is a difficult "surprise" to master.

surprise = _____

The birthday surprise:

a _____ to the _____ _____

      (Set One)   (Set Two)   (Set Three)

Name _____

Careful Notes

In each set of sentences below, find the secret word that "note" replaces. It replaces the same word in all four sentences of a set. However, the secret word is different for each set. After you decode the three secret words, discover how a musician can create a sad mood by completing the sentence at the bottom of the page.

Set One

1. Susan and Joey acted in the school "note."

2. Let's "note" a game of hide and seek.

3. What game shall we "note" at recess?

4. A double meaning is a "note" on words.

note = _____

Set Two

1. It was a "note" infraction of the rules.

2. She can't vote because she's still a "note."

3. My brother Andy played "note" league baseball.

4. It was a "note" injury; all it needed was a small bandage.

note = _____

Set Three

1. The map had a "note" to explain what the symbols meant.

2. The "note" to success is hard work.

3. Dad had an extra "note" made for the car.

4. Chris's piano needed to have a chipped "note" replaced.

note = _____

A musician's way to create a sad mood:

_____ in a _____ _____

    (Set One)   (Set Two)   (Set Three)

Name _____

Pickle Riddle

In each set of sentences below, find the secret word that "pickle" replaces. It replaces the same word in all four sentences of a set. However, the secret word is different for each set. After you decode the three secret words, discover what Aunt Betty wants you to do while she is on vacation by completing the sentence at the bottom of the page.

Set One

1. John and Lynn use "pickle" to wash their dog.

2. Every three days, Henry would "pickle" the flowers.

3. "Pickle" in the ocean has a high salt content.

4. Joe asked for a drink of "pickle."

pickle = _____

Set Two

1. Tom's mother was elected to the "Pickle" of Representatives.

2. Elaine's theater group played to a full "pickle."

3. After school, Doug went to Bill's "pickle" to borrow a book.

4. We have the prettiest "pickle" on the block."

pickle = _____

Set Three

1. Aunt Gilda bought a flowering "pickle" for her backyard.

2. Agent Ziegfried was ordered to "pickle" a microphone on an enemy agent.

3. Robin works at an automobile "pickle."

4. Francine wants to "pickle" a vegetable garden this spring.

pickle = _____

Your job while Aunt Betty is on vacation:

_____ the _____ _____

(Set One)　　　　　　　(Set Two)　　　　(Set Three)

Name _____ 15

Adventures with Logic, copyright © 1985

A Platter of Plates

Decode each of the personalized license plates below. Then, write a description of the type of person whose job or personality it might fit.

1. | **TNTFRND** | _____

2. | **LB 4 LB** | _____

3. | **X AGER8** | _____

4. | **10S NE1** | _____

5. | **ED U K8** | _____

Design a license plate, with seven letters or less, for each of the following people:

1. An energetic dancer

2. A medical student

3. A friend everyone likes

4. An Olympic champion

5. Your best friend

Adventures with Logic, copyright © 1985

Car Appeal

Decode each of the personalized license plates below. Then, write a description of the type of person whose job or personality it might fit.

1. | 4STLOVR | _____

2. | PRIV8 I | _____

3. | W8WACHR | _____

4. | C I 2 I | _____

5. | B4ULEAP | _____

Design a license plate, with seven letters or less, for each of the following people:

1. A parent

2. A basketball player

3. A scuba diver

4. A ghost story writer

5. Yourself

Bottled Code

Three coded messages washed ashore in a bottle. Then, a second bottle appeared with three keys to decode the messages. Using scratch paper, figure out which key goes with each message. Then write the decoded message on the line under each code.

Coded Messages

1. EHLI,P'MTARPEPODANINSALNDIWTOHNYLIMLKSAHEKSOTDIRNK

_____

_____

_____

2. FTHNLYEWVTGEIRGTTNOLWVHRS,BUGGETYWRTFHNDTROUL

_____

_____

_____

3. UNLEJSSJEWGJTEHEJPLSOJNOJEWWIJLLOPJNEJPUJNAIJECCREJMAPARLOR

_____

_____

_____

Decoding Keys

A. Switch each vowel with the letter that comes after it. Then, put spaces between the words.

B. Switch every "J" once with the second letter after it. Then, replace each "J" with a space.

C. Replace these letters, in this order:
   "W" becomes "A,"
   "F" becomes "W,"
   "O" becomes "F,"
   "H" becomes "O,"
   "E" becomes "H,"
   "T" becomes "E,"
   and "G" becomes "T." Then, put spaces between the words.

Name _____

Post Code

Uncle Mort always sends postcards written in code. Using scratch paper, follow the instructions to decode the message. Then, write the decoded message on the lines at the bottom of the page.

Postcard

L P N D X N P H X O S B Y X N Y G R Y T O Z X I T

X I S Y X O S A X P T F P L L X W P

Y E P L X Y E X I N F X G P W T I H P X U T

B Y N X G I S Y Y N Z L O X P S T X Y H

S Y E Y X H C X I S Y X O S A X P T N U D Y R S T N O D Z

Decoding Instructions

1. Switch every "X" with the second letter after it.

2. Switch every vowel, except for "Y," with the letter before it.

3. Replace these letters in the following order:
   "E" becomes "P,"
   "Y" becomes "E,"
   "A" becomes "Y,"
   "O" becomes "A,"
   and "P" becomes "O."

4. Replace each "X" with a space and each "Z" with a period.

5. Replace the first and third "O" on the third line, and the first "O" on the fifth line with a "P."

The Message:

_____

_____

_____

_____

_____

Adventures with Logic, copyright © 1985

Roman Rules

Three pairs of Roman numerals are listed on the bottom of the page. Transform the first numeral into the second numeral by applying the rules listed below. Write the rule applied for each step you perform. Try to complete the transformation with as few steps as possible. The first pair has been completed for you. (As you may have guessed by now, many of these Roman numerals are imaginary.)

Rules

1. After an "I," you may place a numeral "V," "X," "L," "C," or "M."

2. Before a "V," you may place any numeral except "I" or "X."

3. When two "V's" appear in a row, you may eliminate a numeral on either side of the "V's."

4. An "I" may be placed between any double numerals. (For example, "XX" may be changed to "XIX.")

5. When "VV" begins a numeral which ends in "M" or "C," you may eliminate both "V's."

1. VII to CM

step	rule
VIIM	1
VIICM	1
VVIICM	2
VVICM	3
VVCM	5
CM	5

2. XI to CIC

step	rule

3. MMI to VIV

step	rule

Name _____

Sporting Chance

The clues below are plays on words. They hint at the names of seven different sports which can be made from the list of letters below. Some of the sports are unusual. Each clue also lists the number of letters in the answer. Cross out each letter as you use it. The first one has been done for you.

a, a, b̶, b, c, c, c, c, c, c, d, e, e, e, e, e, f, g̶,
g, h, i̶, i, i, i, i, k, m, n̶, n, n, n, n, n, n, ø̶, o,
o, o, q, q, r, r, r, s, s, s, s, t, t, t, t, u, u, x̶.

Clues

1. The sport you do when you are packing to move.

   (six letters) _____boxing_____

2. The sport you should never do to your sister.

   (six letters) _____

3. The summer sport found in the vegetable garden.

   (six letters) _____

4. The sport that chirps at twilight.

   (seven letters) _____

5. The sport that won't keep your hands warm.

   (nine letters) _____

6. The sport that keeps horses in the corral.

   (seven letters) _____

7. The sport that answers the problem of five plus five.

   (six letters) _____

8. What a sporting frog says when agreeing with someone.

   (seven letters) _____

Adventures with Logic, copyright © 1985

Password

In order to gain access to the computer program, you need to decode the password. In each set of words below, one or two letters have been replaced by numbers. The same number always stands for the same letter. Decode the numbers and fill in the blanks at the bottom of the page to discover the password. The first set has been done for you.

Set A	Decode 2	Set B	Decode 3	Decode 4
wr2ng	a, o, u.	3ever	_____	_____
b2res	a, o.	mi3es	_____	_____
d2es	o, u.	sta4e	_____	_____
to2l	o, l.	bri34	_____	_____
	2 = o		3 = _____	4 = _____

Set C	Decode 5	Set D	Decode 1	Decode 6
5ater	_____	sla6	_____	_____
s5at	_____	6oke	_____	_____
5ase	_____	1a6or	_____	_____
star5	_____	rh61e	_____	_____
	5 = _____		1 = _____	6 = _____

Set E	Decode 7		
wi7e	_____	live7	_____
7ole	_____	7ender	_____
ri7e	_____	7 = _____	

PASSWORD: _____ _____ _____ _____ _____ _____ _____
           1   2   3   4   5   6   7

Name _____

Adventures with Logic, copyright © 1985

Word Transform

For each pair of words below, change the first word into the second word, by changing one letter at a time. Each change must create a real word. The first pair has been done for you.

1. Port to ship

port

sort

soot

shot

shop

ship

2. mile to yard

3. city to town

4. foot to race

5. clown to flips

6. bait to hook

DEDUCTION

These activities consist of simple riddles and complex puzzles. To solve the more difficult problems, students must apply rules, discern relevant information, and carefully record relationships.

And Riddles, But Riddles, Camp-Out, But And Riddles, Or Riddles, More Or Riddles, Camp Chores, Unless Riddles, More Unless Riddles, If-Then Riddles, and If-Then II: Students will practice the use of logical connectives. Although students are familiar with connectives, they often do not use them correctly. The activities are best presented in order, over the course of several weeks. Students can be encouraged to consciously use the connectives in class discussions.

Weight Room, Disk Jockey, Play-Off, Beach Scene, Family Reunion, Video Rodeo, and Party Favors: Students will solve puzzles which involve a complicated relationship of clues. The words "no," "at least," and "both" are stressed in these activities. Students can work alone on the activities or in pairs. A class discussion after the exercise would be useful for instructing students in several types of problem solving strategies.

And Riddles

The word "and" is the most common logical connecting word. It is used to combine two clauses.

Example

El Salvador is a country.

San Salvador is a city.

You can connect these two true statements with an "and."

El Salvador is a country and San Salvador is a city.

When an "and" statement is true, *both* of the statements must be true.

Example

Ann likes cherry pie and Liz likes apple pie.

From this sentence, you know what kind of pie both people like.

Solve the riddles below. It is sometimes easier when you break the "and" statements into two smaller statements.

Riddle 1

1. Nick made TV dinners for his younger brother and two younger sisters.

2. He made Salisbury steak, fried chicken, and spaghetti.

3. Phil would not eat the chicken, and Nick did not give him spaghetti.

4. Gretchen would eat anything, and Debbie would not eat spaghetti.

Phil ate _____.   Gretchen ate _____.

Debbie ate _____.

Riddle 2

1. Five friends ran a fifty-yard dash.

2. Sandy finished in 6.4 seconds, and Leslie finished faster.

3. Chris finished behind Sandy, and ahead of Robin.

4. Kelly ran 0.3 seconds faster than Leslie.

Who won the race? _____.

Who came in last? _____.

But Riddles

We use the word "but" to join two statements. Logically, it means the same thing as "and," but it also suggests that there is a conflict between the two statements it joins.

Example

It is snowing outside, but Freddy is only wearing swim trunks.

From this sentence, you know that it is snowing and you know that Freddy is only wearing swim trunks.

The use of "but" instead of "and" in the example above emphasizes that the two statements are unusual together. Now, solve the riddles below.

Riddle 1

1. There were three surfboards on the sand; a red one, a blue one, and a green one.

2. Murray waxed his board and his brother's board, but not the red one.

3. Sally likes her surfboard, but prefers David's green board.

David's board is _____.   Sally's board is _____.

Murray's board is _____.

Riddle 2

Four friends are walking to a movie show, but must decide which film to see. The choices are a horror film, a drama, a comedy, and a musical.

1. John likes all movies, but he isn't in the mood for a horror film.

2. Debbie refuses to see a drama, but will watch anything else.

3. Mitch likes comedies, but says that the musical had good reviews.

4. The musical is playing seven miles away, but the other shows are within walking distance.

Which movie is the best choice? _____

Camp-Out

Six friends went backpacking. Read the clues below to figure out which sleeping bag belongs to whom. Then write the name of each camper next to the correct bag.

Clues

1. Bruce and Walter are brothers, and are sleeping as far away from each other as possible.

2. Peter is next to Paul, but not next to Allen.

3. Allen is playing cards with Walter, who is closest to the logs.

4. Peter is a good friend of Bruce, but is not sleeping next to him.

5. Mark is next to Peter, but not next to Bruce.

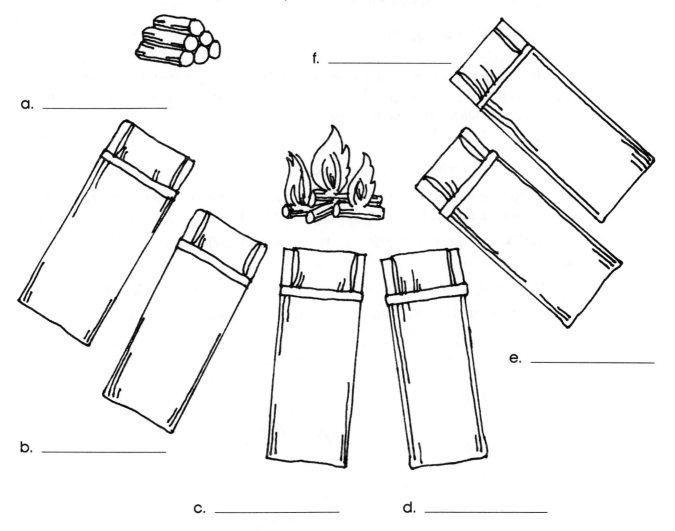

a. _____

f. _____

b. _____

c. _____

d. _____

e. _____

But And Riddles

TV Dispute

In the Field's house, disputes over which channel to watch on TV are settled by a vote. Tonight, the choice is between a situation comedy on channel three, and an old movie mystery on channel five. There are five voting members. Read the clues below and figure out which channel was chosen.

Clues

1. Mother voted for one channel, and Father voted for the other channel.

2. Janice likes old movies, but she voted for channel three anyway.

3. Denise voted for channel five, but Craig did not.

   Which channel was chosen? _____

Cards and Bragging

Four grandparents are playing cards and bragging about their grandchildren. Read the clues and, on the diagram below, write the name of each grandparent and the grandchild he or she is bragging about. Grandpa Mitch's position has been labeled for you.

Clues

1. Grandpa Mitch is dealing clockwise, and he gets the last card.

2. Grandpa Stan is bragging about Susan's swimming ability, and he does not notice that he has been dealt the first card.

3. Two partners, sitting across the table from each other, brag about Shelly and Kim.

4. Grandpa Mitch has never met Kim, but he knows Richard, Celia's grandson.

5. Kim's grandfather has the same name as Celia's grandson.

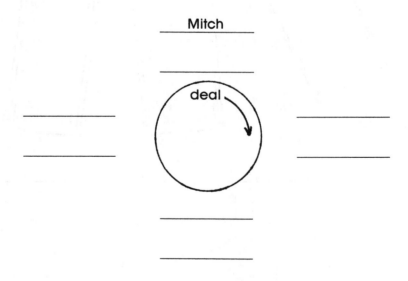

Name _____

Or Riddles

"Or," like "and," is a common logical connective. However, when an "or" statement is true, one of the two clauses that it connects must be true.

Example 1

Greg caught the fish, or Cindy caught the fish.

From this sentence, you know that someone caught the fish. However, you do not know who caught it.
If you are able to discover that one of the clauses is false, then you know that the other clause must be true.

Example 2

Jeff went swimming at the park, or his father went swimming.

Jeff stayed home all day.

Because you know that Jeff did not go swimming, you know that his father went swimming.

Now, solve the riddles below.

Riddle 1

1. Becky rode her bike to school, or her dad drove her to school.

2. Her dad was washing the car when Becky left for school.

How did Becky get to school? _____

Riddle 2

1. Elaine reprogrammed the computer, or Asher broke it.

2. The computer was not broken, or the teacher did the grades by hand.

3. The teacher did the grades by hand.

What happened to the computer? _____

Riddle 3

1. At the park, Blanche rode on the roller coaster, or Willie won a stuffed elephant.

2. No stuffed elephants were given as prizes, or Nancy ate pink cotton candy.

3. Nancy eats only candied apples or no sweets at all.

Did Blanche ride the roller coaster? _____

Did Willie win the stuffed elephant? _____

More Or Riddles

Remember the rules for "or" statements.

     I. In a true "or" statement, at least one of the clauses must be true.

     II. In a true "or" statement, if you discover that one of the clauses is false, the other clause must be true.

Now, solve these "or" riddles.

Top Dog

1. Sniffles or Ginger is the smartest dog on the block.

2. Sniffles is the smartest dog on the block, or Harlow is the fattest cat on the block.

3. No other cat on the block is fatter than Caine.

Who's the smartest dog on the block? _____

Diet Dilemma

1. Either Robert or Michael diets more than any other wrestling team member.

2. Robert does not diet, or else he has too much free time.

3. Robert does not have enough free time.

Who diets the most on the wrestling team? _____

Snake Plans

1. The snake basked in the sun all day, or he hid under a rock.

2. The snake hid under a rock, or a hunter caught him.

3. The snake was not caught.

Where did the snake spend the day? _____

30   Name _____

Camp Chores

At camp, each cabin has to work on a different cleanup job. Read the clues below. Then, on the grid at the bottom of the page, place an "X" to match each cabin with the correct chore. You can use a "O" to mark a match that you know is incorrect, and you can indicate "maybe" matches. The first clue has been marked for you to demonstrate how to mark a "maybe" match.

Clues

1. Cabin 3 wants to clean the pool or wash the showers.
2. Cabin 4 does not want to set tables or sweep cabins.
3. Cabin 1 likes sweeping cabins or straightening out the art room.
4. The horses will allow only Cabin 5 or Cabin 6 to groom them.
5. Cabin 5 wants to wash the showers in order to have a water fight.
6. Cabin 2 wants to set tables.

	Cabin 1	Cabin 2	Cabin 3	Cabin 4	Cabin 5	Cabin 6
Clean Pool			X if Shower = 0			
Wash Showers			X if Pool=0			
Set Tables						
Sweep Cabins						
Groom Horses						
Straighten out Art Room						

Adventures with Logic, copyright © 1985

Unless Riddles

Logically speaking, "unless" means the same thing as "or."

Example 1

Unless Greg caught the fish, Cindy caught the fish.

From this statement, you know that one of the two people caught the fish. Just as with "or" statements, if one of the clauses in an "unless" statement is false, then the other clause must be true.

Example 2

Unless Janet marries Bailey, Betty will marry him.

Betty will not marry Bailey.

From these two statements, you know that Janet will marry Bailey.

Solve the riddles below. You will notice that "unless" does not have to be between the two clauses.

Kad's Caper

1. Unless it rains, Lenny Kad will play soccer.

2. Unless Lenny plays soccer, he will go to the dance tonight.

3. Lenny wants to go to the dance tonight.

Is Lenny hoping for rain or shine? _____

The Lost Expedition

1. The Lost Expedition will march forever, unless Robert finds the compass.

2. Unless Barbara asks Robert to check his knapsack, he will never find the compass.

3. Unless Robert and Barbara stop fighting, she will never ask Robert to check his knapsack.

4. Unless Robert finds the compass, he and Barbara will never stop fighting.

What will happen to the Lost Expedition? _____

Name _____

Adventures with Logic, copyright © 1985

More Unless Riddles

The rules for "unless" statements are the same as the rules for "or" statements.

     I. In a true "unless" statement, at least one of the clauses must be true.

    II. In a true "unless" statement, if one clause is false, then the other clause must be true.

Solve the riddles below.

Ski Driver

1. George will drive everyone to the ski slope, or Cami will take the bus.

2. Unless Cami gets a ride in a car, her mother will not let her go skiing.

3. Unless Sandra goes skiing, George will not drive.

For Cami to go skiing, Sandra must _____

Exhibit A

1. Unless Andrea finishes her painting, the art exhibit will not be complete.

2. Andrea will finish her painting, unless the lighting is poor.

3. The lighting will be good, unless it rains.

It will rain or the art exhibit will _____

Animals On Parade

1. The parade will go down either Fifth Street or Third Street.

2. The parade will go down Third Street, unless the dancing bears are too tired.

3. The dancing bears will be tired, unless there is a rest day before the parade.

Unless there is a day of rest before the parade, the parade will go down _____ Street.

Adventures with Logic, copyright © 1985

If-Then Riddles

"If-then" statements are tricky. The first clause (the "if" clause) is called a conditional. It describes a condition. The second clause (the "then" clause) is called a consequence. When the conditional—the "if" clause—is true, then the consequence—the "then" clause—must be true.

Example 1

If it is cloudy, then I need an umbrella.

It is cloudy.

From these two facts, you know that an umbrella is required.

Example 2

If it is raining, then my laundry is wet.

My laundry is not wet.

From these two statements, you know that it is not raining. When the "then" clause of an "if-then" statement is false, then the "if" clause must be false.

Solve the "if-then" riddles below.

Race-Off

1. If Frank ran faster than Archie, then Frank won the race.
2. Louis won the race.

Who ran faster—Frank or Archie? _____

Forward Positions

1. If Gloria plays center, then Jodi will play guard.
2. If Jodi plays guard, then Karen will play forward.
3. If Karen plays forward, then Jenny will also play forward.
4. If Gloria plays guard, then Susan and Mickey will play forwards.
5. Gloria will play center.

Who will play the two forward positions? _____

If-Then II

"If-then" statements follow these rules:

    I. When the "if" clause is true, the "then" clause is true.

    II. When the "then" clause is false, the "if" clause must be false.

However, there is another possible situation: when the "if" clause is false, the then clause may still be true!

Example

    If it is sunny, Beth will go to the beach.

    It is not sunny.

Although it is not sunny, Beth may still go to the beach.

Solve the riddles below.

Football Setup

1. Rich or Dennis will play quarterback.

2. If Rich plays quarterback, then Mike will play tackle.

3. Rich will not play quarterback.

Who will play quarterback? _____   Will Mike play tackle? _____

Figure Eights

1. If Julie goes ice skating, then her friend Jeff will go ice skating.

2. If Jeff goes ice skating, then his sister Angie will go ice skating.

3. Jeff will not go ice skating.

Will Julie go ice skating? _____   Will Angie go ice skating? _____

Ripple Riddle

1. Only three people can go swimming.

2. If George goes swimming, then one person cannot go swimming.

3. If Ann goes swimming, then Lisa will go swimming.

4. If Lisa goes swimming, then Larry will not go swimming.

5. If Larry goes swimming, then George will go swimming.

6. If Ann goes swimming, then one person cannot go swimming.

Which three people can go swimming? _____

Name _____

Adventures with Logic, copyright © 1985

Weight Room

Five athletes are working out in a small weight room. Each athlete is doing a different exercise. Read the clues below. Then, on the grid at the bottom of the page, place an "X" to match each athlete with the correct exercise. You can use an "O" to mark a match that you know is incorrect, and you can indicate "maybe" matches. The first clue has been marked for you to demonstrate how to mark a "maybe" match.

Clues

1. If Rocky is bench pressing, then Wendy is doing squats next to him.
2. If Andy is doing curls, then Tom is not doing leg lifts.
3. If Tom is not doing leg lifts, then June is.
4. If Andy is not doing curls, then Rocky is.
5. If Rocky is not bench pressing, then Wendy is using the pulley.
6. Wendy is not using the pulley.

	Rocky	Andy	Tom	Wendy	June
Bench Press	if x, Wendy = Squats				
Squats				if 0, Rocky ≠ Bench Press	
Curls					
Leg Lifts					
Pulley					

Adventures with Logic, copyright © 1985

Disc Jockey Play-Off

A local radio station auditioned five new disc jockeys for their morning show. Each disc jockey plays a different type of music. Read the clues below. Then, on the grid at the bottom of the page, place an "X" to match each disc jockey with the type of music he or she plays.

Clues

1. Jenny went to the same college as both Slick and the new-wave disc jockey.

2. The rock-and-roll disc jockey auditioned before Jake, who auditioned second.

3. The new-wave disc jockey auditioned last, after Timmy.

4. The rhythm-and-blues disc jockey followed Slick, who was the first to audition.

5. Jenny left before Timmy's audition, because she doesn't like the country music that he plays.

	Jenny	Slick	Betsy	Timmy	Jake
Jazz					
Country					
New Wave					
Rock and Roll					
Rhythm and Blues					

Adventures with Logic, copyright © 1985

Beach Scene

Five friends biked to the beach one Saturday afternoon. Each one took a different route. Read the clues below. Then, on the grid at the bottom of the page, place an "X" to match each biker with the correct sequence of his or her arrival.

Clues

1. Everyone arrived at ten-minute intervals.
2. Howard was the first to arrive.
3. Anna arrived twenty minutes after Veronica.
4. Howard and Steve were playing volleyball when Danny arrived.
5. Danny arrived ten minutes after Anna.
6. Veronica went swimming before Steve arrived with the towels.

	1st	2nd	3rd	4th	5th
Howard					
Anna					
Steve					
Danny					
Veronica					

Name _____

Adventures with Logic, copyright © 1985

Family Reunion

At the Brook's family reunion, Grandma Viola asked her five grandchildren what they wanted to be when they grew up. Read the clues below. Decide which two pairs of children are brothers and sisters. Then, on the grid at the bottom of the page, place an "X" to match each child with his or her desired profession.

Clues

1. Each child wants to be something different.

2. Ann's brother wants to be a doctor.

3. Ron decided not to become a farmer, although his cousin decided to become one.

4. Ed's sister wants to be a dentist.

5. Ann and Mary are cousins.

6. Mary's brother wants to be an actor.

7. Ann does not want to be a dentist.

8. The boy without a sister wants to be a lawyer.

9. Ann approves of her brother Larry's choice.

	Ann	Ron	Ed	Mary	Larry
Doctor					
Farmer					
Dentist					
Actor					
Lawyer					

Name _____

Adventures with Logic, copyright © 1985

Video Rodeo

Five friends competed in five video games. Read the clues below. Then, on the grid at the bottom of the page, write the position each player finished in each event.

Clues

1. In each event, there was a first, second, third, fourth, and fifth finisher.
2. No one won more than two games, and there were no ties.
3. The winner of Spiderweb scored last in all the other games.
4. Michelle placed third in Trucker, ahead of both Creed and Marisa.
5. Marisa won Burnout but finished second in Fast Lane.
6. Jeremy won two games, the only two games in which Michelle finished third.
7. Michelle finished fifth in at least one game.
8. Marisa had one more fourth place finish than Michelle had.
9. One person finished second in four of the games, and won a fifth game.

	Jeremy	Denise	Marisa	Michelle	Creed
Spiderweb					
Trucker					
Fast Lane					
Burnout					
Night Flight					

Name _____

Party Favors

Christine had a small birthday party, and she gave out party favors. Read the clues below. Then, on the grid at the bottom of the page, place an "X" to match each person with the correct favors. You can use an "O" to mark a match that you know is incorrect.

Clues

1. Some friends got two favors, but no one got more than two.

2. No boy got something to eat.

3. At least two guests got candied apples.

4. No one had both candied apples and another thing to eat.

5. Amy refused to trade her fudge for Corey's trick candles.

6. Only one friend got a helium balloon, and he got nothing else.

7. John got two favors.

8. Only the friends with candied apples got puzzle books.

9. Noisemakers were the only favors that both a boy and a girl received.

10. Only two guests received only one favor.

	Sarah	Lila	Amy	John	Corey	Walter
Candied Apples						
Noisemakers						
Trick Candles						
Fudge						
Helium Balloons						
Puzzle Books						

Name _____

Adventures with Logic, copyright © 1985

CREATIVE LOGIC

These activities combine logic with creativity, an essential element of advanced logic use. The answers are, in part, open-ended, and much of the value of the activities is in allowing students to test the constraints of the directions.

Cleverisms: Students explore how new words come about. This can be applied to vocabulary lessons as well as creative writing assignments.

Create-a-Thing, Mystery Phrases, and Word Wind: Students will look at words and objects in new ways. This is the way much scientific invention comes about.

Fill-in the Story and The Story's the Thing: Students will develop stories within the constraints of given sentences. After doing these activities and reading the stories aloud, students can explore the way sequence, perception, and choice of information can dramatically transform the meaning of a story.

Time Capsule: Students will choose symbols to represent large concepts. This activity can help students understand symbolism in literature and propaganda.

Cleverisms

Sometimes a new word is invented to describe a new idea, an invention, or a discovery. Every word was once a new word. Below is a list of a few words and their roots.

Word	Prefix	Meaning	Root	Meaning
neologism (a new word)	neo-	new	-logism	word
transport (to carry somewhere)	trans-	across	-port	carry
circumlocution (to speak around the main subject)	circum-	around	-locution	speaking
microscope (a device for examining small things)	micro-	small	-scope	examine
isomorphic (having the same form)	iso-	same	-morphic	form

Make up three new words, using parts of words that you are familiar with. Then, write their definitions.

Word 1: _____

Word 2: _____

Word 3: _____

Now, in the space below, write a paragraph using the three new words.

_____

_____

_____

_____

_____

Adventures with Logic, copyright © 1985

Create-a-Thing

Sometimes, the best inventions are those that use old objects in new ways. Below are two groups of objects. Design a device that does something useful, using the objects in each group and any other objects that you choose. You may draw or describe your invention, but you must also describe how it works.

Invention 1: a boot, a light bulb, and string

_____

_____

_____

Invention 2: a wheel, a fork, and a parrot

_____

_____

_____

Name _____

Mystery Phrases

Each of these strange word-cartoons illustrates a familiar phrase. Beneath each cartoon, write the expression it illustrates.

a. _____

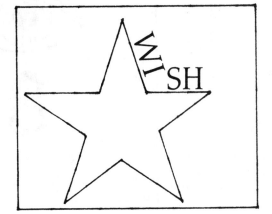

b. _____

c. _____

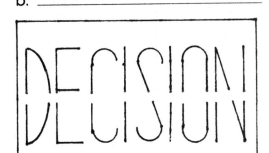

d. _____

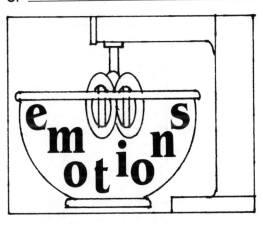

e. _____

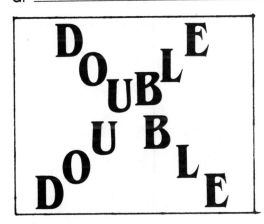

f. _____

Name _____

Adventures with Logic, copyright © 1985

Word Wind

Beneath each word-cartoon, write the expression it illustrates.

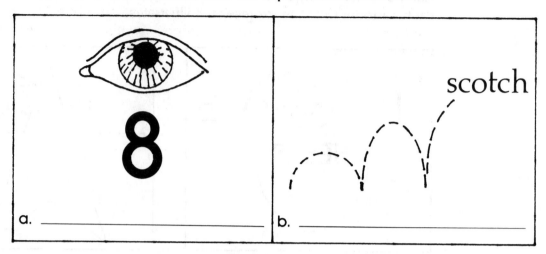

a. _____ b. _____

Draw word-cartoons for each of these sayings.

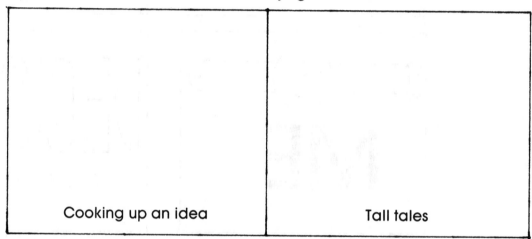

Cooking up an idea   Tall tales

Now, make up your own word-cartoons and see if your friends can guess them.

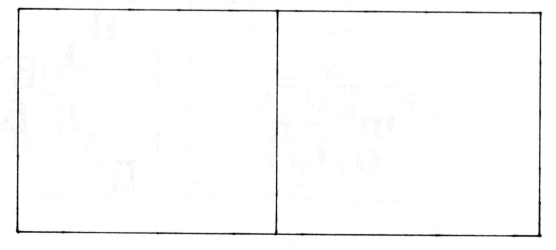

Name _____

Adventures with Logic, copyright © 1985

Fill-in the Story

In this short story, the word processor erased everything (including the title), except for the first and last sentences. Reconstruct a possible short story that uses the first and last sentences. It can be any kind of story that you would like to write.

Title: _____

The door creaked as it opened, and I felt a cold, stale gust of wind. _____

_____

_____

_____

_____

_____

_____

_____

_____

_____

_____

_____ Never again will I have such a birthday party.

Name _____

Adventures with Logic, copyright © 1985

The Story's the Thing

The word processor malfunctioned and erased everything from this short story, except for three sentences: the first one, the last one, and one in the middle. Reconstruct a story around the three sentences. Then, give the story a title.

Title: _____

We were wondering where we would get the money. _____

_____

_____

_____

_____

_____

Dishes were piling up in the sink. _____

_____

_____

_____

_____

_____

_____

_____

_____ My mother told us to play outside for the rest of the month.

48   Name _____

Time Capsule

Hundreds of years from now, people will wonder what our lives were like. Design the contents of a time capsule (a large, airtight, waterproof container) for people to discover five hundred years from now. Five categories are listed below. Decide on objects that would represent each category. Then, for each object, write why you think it is a good choice.

Object 1: your country. _____

_____

_____

Object 2: your city. _____

_____

_____

_____

Object 3: your favorite music. _____

_____

_____

_____

Object 4: your weekends. _____

_____

_____

_____

Object 5: yourself. _____

_____

_____

Name _____

Adventures with Logic, copyright © 1985

GAMES FOR PAIRS

These are all games requiring strategy.

Digit Counter and Coin Computer: These are guessing games, in which the reply to a guess gives information that aids in the next guess. This is analogous to the way scientists develop hypotheses and conduct research.

Ten-X and Tric-Trac-Trow: Students will devise appropriate strategies for achieving the stated objectives. The games are simple enough so that students can plan their best moves with confidence. Ten-X is followed by questions, so that students can analyze their strategies.

Digit Counter

This is a strategy guessing game. One player makes up a number and the other player tries to guess it.

Rules

1. Choose one person to be the guesser and the other to be the counter.

2. The counter writes a four-digit number on a piece of paper without showing it to the guesser. No two numbers in the four-digit number may be the same.

3. The guesser writes a four-digit number in the "guess" column of the chart below.

4. The counter marks the "tally" column as follows:
   a. For each correct digit in the right place, mark an "X."
   b. For each correct digit in the wrong place, mark an "O."
   c. If a digit is incorrect, draw a line through the box.

5. The guessing continues until the correct four-digit number is guessed. The counter writes the number in the tally column.

6. The players switch roles and play another round. The winner is the player with the fewest guesses after four rounds.

Tally Chart

Turn	Round 1 Guess	Round 1 Tally	Round 2 Guess	Round 2 Tally	Round 3 Guess	Round 3 Tally	Round 4 Guess	Round 4 Tally
1.								
2.								
3.								
4.								
5.								
6.								
7.								
8.								
9.								
10.								
11.								
12.								

Name _____

Coin Computer

Player A

Do Not Show This Page to Your Opponent Until the Game is Over.

This is a strategy guessing game. For rounds 1 and 3, you will be the computer. For rounds 2 and 4, you will be the guesser. Follow the directions exactly. You will need a coin.

Directions

1. The computer places a coin, either heads or tails up, out of view of the guesser.

2. The guesser guesses "heads" or "tails."

3. The computer tells the guesser which side of the coin is up, and the guesser records the result on his or her scorecard below.

4. The computer turns the coin over or leaves it the same, depending on the directions for that round.

5. The round continues until the guesser discovers the pattern and makes five correct guesses in a row.

6. The winner is the player with the fewest guesses after four rounds.

Round 1: You are the computer. Begin with tails. When a guess is correct, turn the coin over. When a guess is wrong, do not turn the coin.

Round 2: You are the guesser. Mark your scorecard below.

#	Guess	Answer	#	Guess	Answer	#	Guess	Answer	#	Guess	Answer
1.			6.			11.			16.		
2.			7.			12.			17.		
3.			8.			13.			18.		
4.			9.			14.			19.		
5.			10.			15.			20.		

Round 3: You are the computer. Begin with heads. Turn the coin to tails only for guessing turns which are multiples of three. Turn the coin to heads for all other guesses.

Round 4: You are the guesser. Mark your scorecard below.

#	Guess	Answer	#	Guess	Answer	#	Guess	Answer	#	Guess	Answer
1.			6.			11.			16.		
2.			7.			12.			17.		
3.			8.			13.			18.		
4.			9.			14.			19.		
5.			10.			15.			20.		

Name _____

Coin Computer

Player B

Do Not Show This Page to Your Opponent Until the Game is Over.

This is a strategy guessing game. For rounds 1 and 3, you will be the guesser. For rounds 2 and 4, you will be the computer. Follow the directions exactly. You will need a coin.

Directions

1. The computer places a coin, either heads or tails up, out of view of the guesser.

2. The guesser guesses "heads" or "tails."

3. The computer tells the guesser which side of the coin is up, and the guesser records the result on his or her scorecard below.

4. The computer turns the coin over or leaves it the same, depending on the directions for that round.

5. The round continues until the guesser discovers the pattern and makes five correct guesses in a row.

6. The winner is the player with the fewest guesses after four rounds.

Round 1: You are the guesser. Mark your scorecard below.

#	Guess	Answer	#	Guess	Answer	#	Guess	Answer	#	Guess	Answer
1.			6.			11.			16.		
2.			7.			12.			17.		
3.			8.			13.			18.		
4.			9.			14.			19.		
5.			10.			15.			20.		

Round 2: You are the computer. Begin with tails. After a guess of tails, turn the coin over for the next turn. Do not turn the coin if the guess is heads.

Round 3: You are the guesser. Mark your scorecard below.

#	Guess	Answer	#	Guess	Answer	#	Guess	Answer	#	Guess	Answer
1.			6.			11.			16.		
2.			7.			12.			17.		
3.			8.			13.			18.		
4.			9.			14.			19.		
5.			10.			15.			20.		

Round 4: You are the computer. Begin with heads. When a guess is wrong, turn the coin over. When a guess is correct, do not turn the coin.

Name _____

Ten-X

This is a strategy game for two players. Each player takes a turn circling either one, two or three "X's," beginning with the one on the far left and working towards the right. Whoever circles the final "X" loses. Repeat the game with the other person starting first. Continue switching the starting player for each game until six games have been completed.

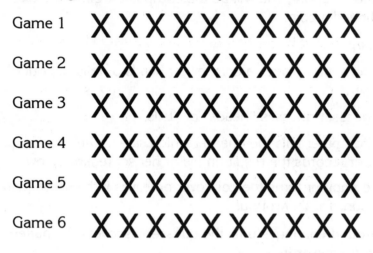

Game 1 X X X X X X X X X X

Game 2 X X X X X X X X X X

Game 3 X X X X X X X X X X

Game 4 X X X X X X X X X X

Game 5 X X X X X X X X X X

Game 6 X X X X X X X X X X

After completing the games, work with your partner and write the answers to these strategy questions.

1. Who has the advantage, the player going first or second? _____

2. Which is the best first move—circling one, two or three? _____

3. If the first player circles three "X's," what is the second player's

   best move? _____

4. If the first player circles two and the second player circles two, what should

   the first player do next to win? _____

5. If seven "X's" remain and both players make the best moves, who will

   win—the player with the next turn or the opponent? _____

   If five "X's" remain? _____

Name _____

Tric-Trac-Trow

This is a strategy board game for two players. Players take turns drawing one of five shapes in the squares of a board, five squares on a side. The player who draws a shape next to—or at a diagonal to—the same shape, loses.

The Five Shapes Are:

Example 1

Examine the board below of a game in progress. Three squares are labeled for identification.

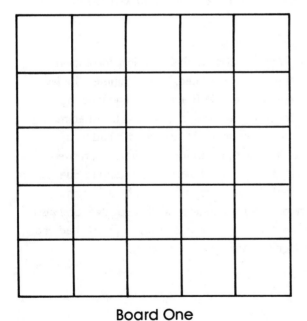

Explanation

a. In box 1, any shape except a △ would lose.

b. In box 2, any shape would lose.

c. In box 3, any shape except a △ would be safe.

Play the game with all five shapes on board one, and with only the first three shapes on board two. Then, you can make your own boards and continue to play.

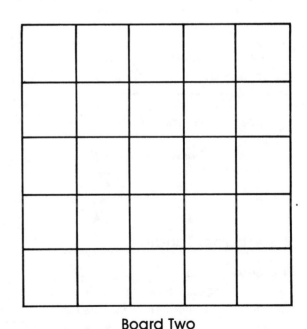

Board One

Board Two

ANSWER KEY

SEQUENCING, SETS, AND ANALOGIES

Moving Day (possible solution)

Vicki's Jobs

Carry in books	10
Set up lamps	20
Set up chairs	20
Shelve dishes	20

Two-mover Jobs

Move piano	20
Move sofa	10
Move dining-room table	20

Jerry's Jobs

Set up bed and headboard	30
Hang paintings	40

(Because of rule #4, books must be first and the dining-room table must be last.)

The Tool Tour (possible solution)

Monday	Tuesday	Wednesday	Thursday
2	3	4	5
N.Y.	N.Y.	N.Y.	travel
9	10	11	12
Chicago	Chicago	Chicago	travel
16	17	18	19
Denver	Denver	Denver	travel
23	24	25	26
travel	Phoenix	Phoenix	Phoenix

Friday	Saturday	Sunday
6	7	8
Nashville	Nashville	travel
13	14	15
Kansas C.	Kansas C.	travel
20	21	22
S.F.	S.F.	S.F.
27	28	29
travel	L.A.	L.A.

Newspaper Tangle

The Space Shuttle
NASA expects, once again, to launch the Space Shuttle near dawn this Thursday. The earlier computer problems that threatened to delay the launch have been fixed. "Everything, including the weather, looks good," said launch engineer Marshall Peters. The Space Shuttle will be taking photographs of the sun for scientists to study. The photos might help show a relationship between sunspots and weather patterns.

The Weather Satellite
A weather satellite is malfunctioning as a result of a computer error, the Weather Service announced today. The satellite provides pictures of the southwestern United States, and is important for predicting changes in air temperature and pressure. The Weather Service believes the malfunction can be fixed in the next few days. Until then, balloons and other older methods will be used. "At least this isn't the rainy season," commented one meteorologist.

Twisted Stories

Shopping Center Fire
Early this morning, before the stores opened, a fire broke out in the Center City shopping mall. Fire trucks rushed to the scene, after the fire was discovered by Larry Lansing, a pastry shop owner. Although no people were inside, fire fighters used axes to get to animals trapped in a pet shop. By 10:00 a.m., the flames dwindled, and several volunteers offered temporary shelter for the shop's dogs, cats, snakes, and rabbits. After the fire was out, Mr. Lansing said, "I think I was more frightened than were the trapped pets."

Erupting Volcano
Shortly after 2:00 a.m. this morning, the ancient volcano Quixtola erupted. Within minutes, the lava had spread over a 200-acre area, endangering hundreds of families and countless forest animals. Rescue and observation teams, who had been expecting the eruption for several weeks, moved quickly to evacuate the area. According to Sue Landoni, the evacuation director, by 3:30 a.m., everyone had been successfully relocated. She also reported that many wild deer and squirrels had fled through the nearby town to safety.

ANSWER KEY

Family Set

1. Every human born
2. Example: collies, Saint Bernards and German shepherds
3. Example: lizards, turtles, beetles
4. Games
5. Fathers
6. All mothers must be daughters.
7. No, all daughters are not mothers.
8. Yes, some sons are parents.
9. No, daughters are not sons.

Animal Set

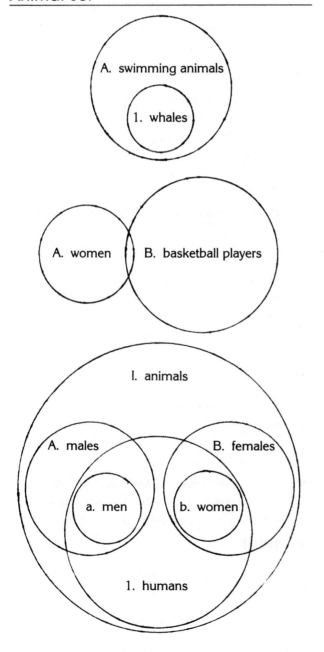

Circle Set

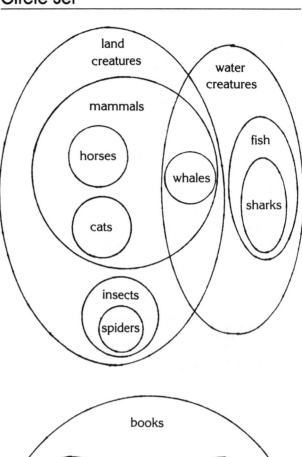

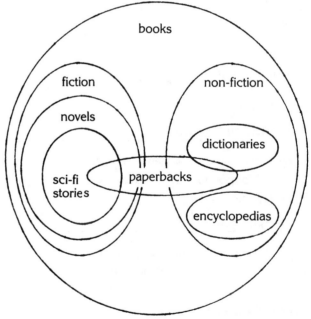

ANSWER KEY

Analogies I

1. track
2. mayor
3. meter
4. county
5. leaves
6. punchline
7. fern
8. sip
9. stalk
10. avalanche

Analogies II

1. blood
2. chess
3. temperature
4. chicken
5. tongue
6. talking
7. car
8. summer

1. act, play
2. mask, fencing
3. monkey, mammal
4. clay, pot
5. tennis, court
6. plate, spaghetti
7. play, park
8. teacher, respect

INFERENCE

Birthday Surprise

ticket, ball game

Careful Notes

play, minor key

Pickle Riddle

water, house plants

A Platter of Plates

1. dynamite friend
2. pound for pound
3. exaggerate
4. tennis anyone
5. educate

Car Appeal

1. forest lover
2. private eye
3. weight watcher
4. see eye to eye
5. before you leap

Bottled Code

Message 1, decoded by key A:
Help I'm trapped on an island with only milkshakes to drink.
Message 2, decoded by key C:
We only have thirteen flavors, but they are wonderful.
Message 3, decoded by key B:
Unless we get help soon we will open up an ice cream parlor.

Post Code

London has been great. It is easy to follow people in fog without being seen. Also the speech is easy to understand.

Roman Rules

2.		given	3.		given
	XI			MMI	
	XIC	1		MMIV	1
	XICC	1		MMIVV	2
	XICIC	4		MMVV	3
	XIVCIC	1		MVV	3
	XIVVCIC	2		VV	3
	XVVCIC	3		VIV	4
	VVCIC	3			
	CIC	5			

Sporting Chance

2. soccer
3. squash
4. cricket
5. badminton
6. fencing
7. tennis
8. croquet

Password

monkeys

Word Transform (possible solutions)

2. mile	3. city	4. foot	5. clown	6. bait
mire	pity	loot	flown	bail
mare	pits	look	flows	ball
care	pots	lock	flops	balk
card	tots	lack	flips	back
yard	tows	lace		hack
	town	race		hock
				hook

DEDUCTION

And Riddles

Riddle 1: Phil ate Salisbury steak, Gretchen ate spaghetti, and Debbie ate fried chicken.
Riddle 2: Kelly won, and Robin came in last.

But Riddles

Riddle 1: David—green, Murray—blue, Sally—red
Riddle 2: Comedy

ANSWER KEY

Camp-Out

a. Walter   b. Allen   c. Mark   d. Peter
e. Paul   f. Bruce

But And Riddles

TV Dispute: channel three
Cards and Bragging:

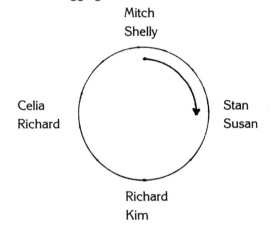

Or Riddles

Riddle 1: She rode her bike.
Riddle 2: Asher broke it.
Riddle 3: Yes. No.

More Or Riddles

Top Dog: Sniffles
Diet Dilemma: Michael
Snake Plans: under a rock

Camp Chores

Cabin 1: sweep cabins   Cabin 4: straighten out art
Cabin 2: set tables   room
Cabin 3: clean pool   Cabin 5: wash showers
                         Cabin 6: groom horses

Unless Riddles

Kad's Caper: rain
The Lost Expedition: They will march forever.

More Unless Riddles

Ski Driver: go skiing.
Exhibit A: be complete.
Animals on Parade: Fifth

If-Then Riddles

Race-Off: Archie
Forward Positions: Karen and Jenny

If-Then II

Football Setup: quarterback—Dennis, Mike may or
                              may not play tackle.
Figure Eights: Julie—no, Angie—maybe
Ripple Riddle: George, Ann, and Lisa

Weight Room

Rocky: bench press   Tom: pulley   June: leg lifts
Andy: curls   Wendy: squats

Disc Jockey Play-Off

Jenny: jazz   Betsy: new wave   Jake: rhythm and
Slick: rock   Timmy: country   blues

Beach Scene

1st: Howard   3rd: Steve   5th: Danny
2nd: Veronica   4th: Anna

Family Reunion

Ann and Larry are brother and sister. Ed and Mary are
brother and sister.
Ann: farmer   Ed: actor   Larry: doctor
Ron: lawyer   Mary: dentist

Video Rodeo

	Jeremy	Denise	Marisa	Michelle	Creed
Spiderweb	3	2	4	5	1
Trucker	1	2	4	3	5
Fast Lane	3	1	2	4	5
Burnout	3	2	1	4	5
Night Flight	1	2	4	3	5

Party Favors

Sarah: candied apples and puzzle books
Lila: candied apples and puzzle books
Amy: noisemakers and fudge
John: noisemakers and trick candles
Corey: trick candles
Walter: helium balloons

ANSWER KEY

CREATIVE LOGIC

Mystery Phrases

a. head over heels in love
b. wish upon a star
c. watch over me
d. split decision
e. mixed emotions
f. double cross

Worn Wind

a. I overate
b. hopscotch

GAMES FOR PAIRS

Ten-X

1. first player
2. three
3. circling one
4. circle one
5. the opponent, the opponent